THE HISTORY OF AFRICAN AMERICANS

From Pyramids, to Poverty, to Pride:

Author **JANICE G. LOGAN**

Art by **ADOFO**

CREATIVE IMAGE PUBLISHING

From Pyramids, to Poverty, to Pride: The History of African Americans. 1st Ed.
Copyright © 2013 & 2014 by Janice G. Logan
All rights reserved. Manufactured in the U.S.A.

No part of this book may be used or reproduced in any manner whatsoever without written permission, except in the case of brief quotations embodied in critical articles and reviews. For information, address Creative Image Publishing.
P.O. Box 532. Moreland. GA 30259

Printed in the United States of America
Cover designed by ADOFO

Library of Congress Catalogue-in-Publications Data

From Pyramids, to Poverty, to Pride: The History of African Americans. 1st Ed.

p. cm.
Includes bibliographical references (p. 90).

I would like to thank all of those who encouraged me as I worked on
From Pyramids, to Poverty, to Pride:
My friend Nyasha Dunkley, who encouraged me to rewrite my play,
which evolved into this book,
my sisters Cherie Moss, and Brenda Hamilton-Moss, for believing in me,
my dear friend Ana Stephens for always lending a word of encouragement,
illustrator Elihu Adofo Bey, for his patience, insight, and perseverance,
my children Barron Logan, Gianina Logan, and Angela Washington,
for their words of encouragement and motivation,
my niece Milana Edwards, for her keen insight,
my husband Marco Logan, for always believing in me and supporting me one hundred percent,
and for historians and writers such as Dr. Ivan Van Sertima
and Runoko Rashidi, whose research helped shed enormous light on the awesome accomplishments
of African American people.

DEDICATION
For my family, the Logan's, Moss's, Morses, Hutchinsons, Cridells, Edwards, Fishers,
Leaches, Treadwells, Colons, Monjes,
Washingtons, Jones's, Davis's, Solomons,
and for every person who has made priceless contributions to our history, down through the ages.

African Americans have a deep, rich history.
Many of the accomplishments of African Americans
have been overlooked,
and, or hidden, until recently.
This book aims to uncover many interesting facts about
Africans/African Americans, and their history.
The author, Janice Logan, uses the words African,
African American, and Black people interchangeably,
when referring to Black people in America.
However, the historical accounts in this book are relevant
to Africans throughout the African diaspora.
Although this is written as a children's book,
it is a book that will interest and inform adults as well.
Reading this book gives the reader
an instant connection with the author, and the historical facts,
which carefully unfold on each page.

Adofo, the illustrator has done a marvelous job of bringing to life,
each fact, statement,
exclamation, declaration, and affirmation.
From Pyramids, to Poverty,
To Pride will leave the reader feeling a plethora of emotions.
It will educate, motivate,
and instill a sense of pride and wonderment,
and leave the reader wanting
to know more about this unmistakable African history.

©Janice G. Logan July 2013

Africa is the cradle of civilization. All life began here.
Africa is a large continent, so large that it can contain
the U.S, China, India, and Argentina.
This vast continent measures 5,500 miles across from east to west,
and from north to south. It is the continent closest to the equator.
Africa is a land of mixed landforms, having mostly desert in the north,
and savannah (grassland in the central areas).
Further south and closer to the equator is where the rainforests (jungles) exist.
But Africa also boasts of beautiful snow capped mountaintops,
which are present at Mt. Kilimanjaro and Mt. Kenya.

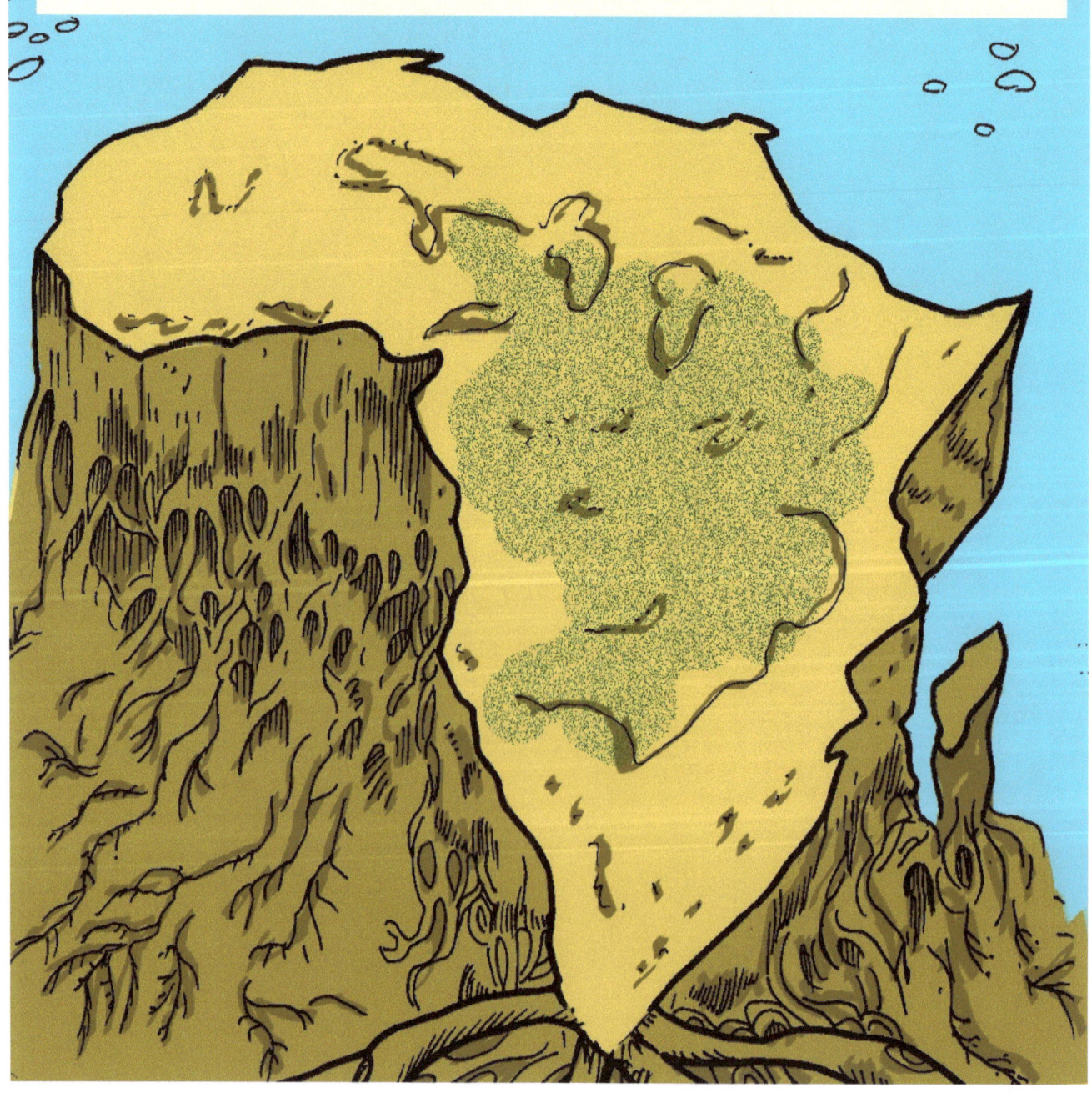

Back in Africa, our people were rulers of mighty kingdoms. Kings and Queens used their God given talents and developed powerful empires, such as Ghana, Songhay, and Timbuktu. Come and take a look at some of the most famous African kings and queens of all time.

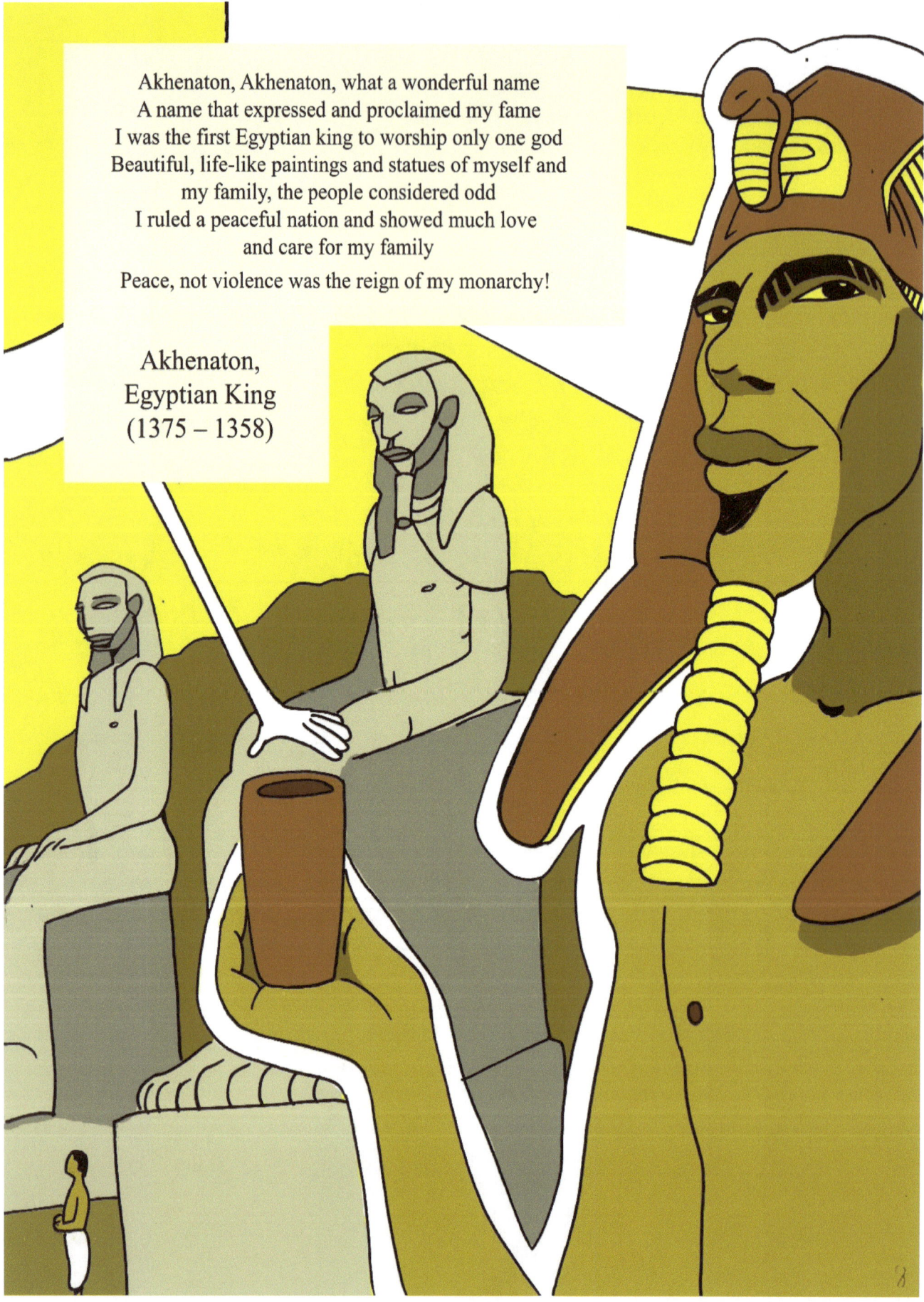

Beautiful Makeda,
Queen of Sheba is one of many names that I bare
Now listen closely to this rhyme, as I inform you about my affair
I was the Queen of both Ethiopia and Saba
I was rich and beautiful, indeed
Upon hearing of the wisdom
and genius of King Solomon of Israel,
A journey to Jerusalem to seek the truth,
was soon my decree
I departed for the Holy City with
almost eight hundred camels, asses,
and mules; loaded with
precious metals, materials, and jewels
Six months with the king,
confirmed all the rumors
For they were all true
King Solomon was the wisest king
to ever live
And now my journey was through.

Makeda, Queen of Sheba (960 B.C.)

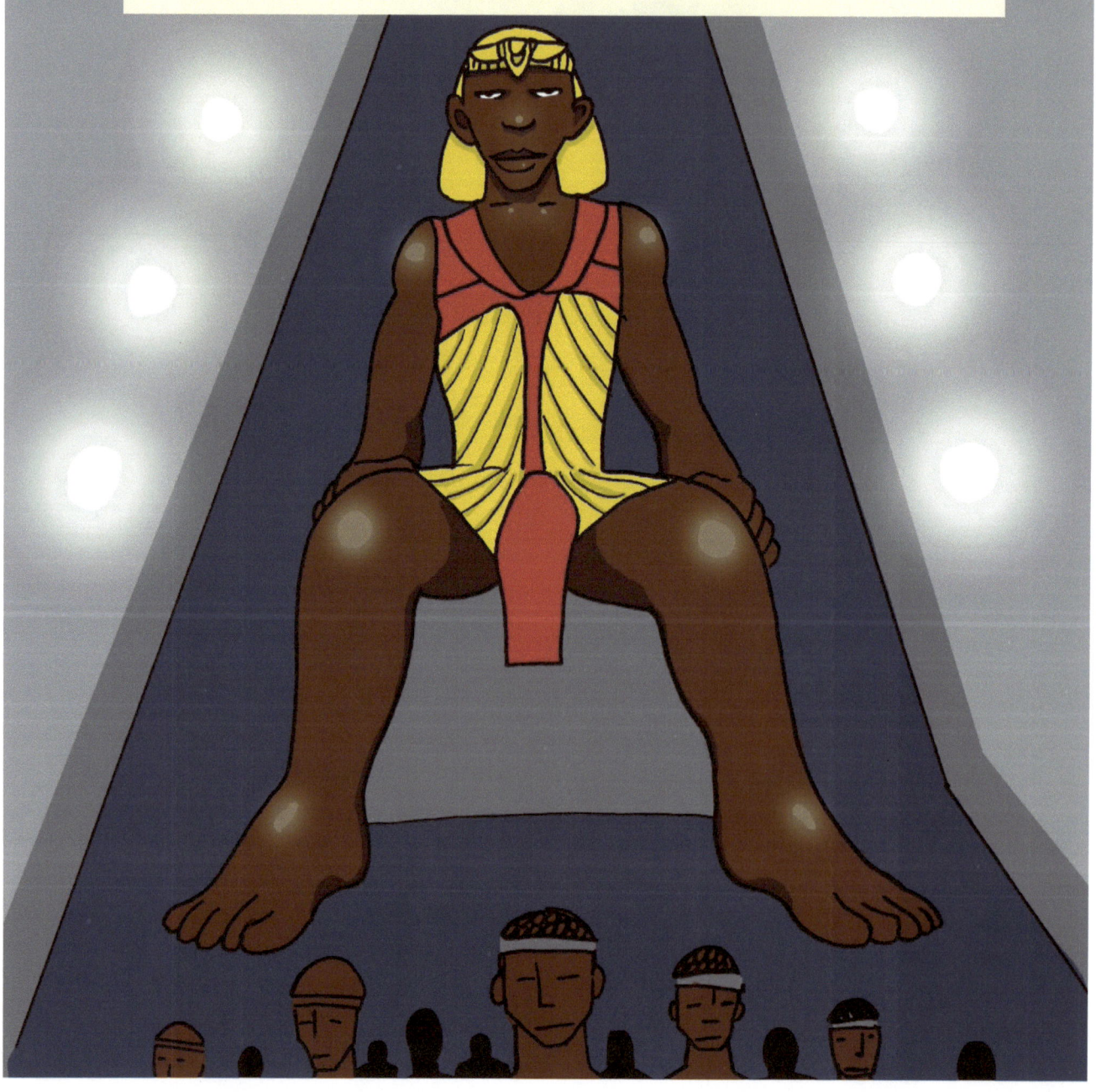

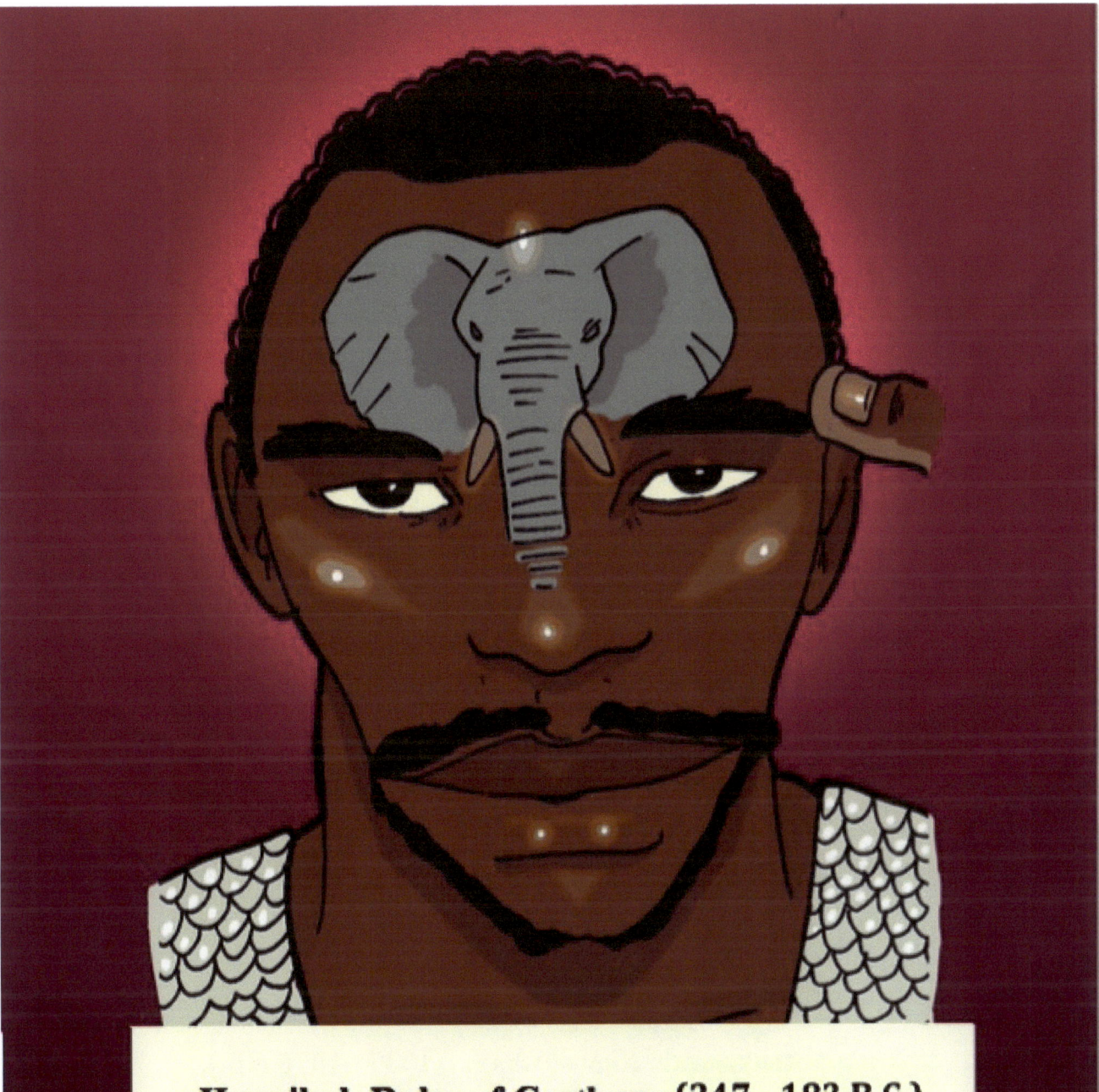

Hannibal, Ruler of Carthage (247 - 183 B.C.)

My name is Hannibal, ruler of Carthage, West Africa.
One of the greatest generals of all times
Although I was young, a mere 25 years old,
I used wisdom and tact to reach my goal
In the middle of the dangerous and very steep Italian Alps
I marched my valiant army on African elephants,
That really gave me clout!
I surrounded the Italian army, and took them by surprise
My fame and reputation traveled far because of their demise.

Tenkamenin King of Ghana (1037 - 1075 A.D.)

Tenkamenin is my name
Ruler of Ghana is my fame
My country reached its height of greatness,
during my reign and rule
Ghana was famous for its rich supply of gold
And wisely managing this impressive trade was my goal
My empire became rich and flourished indeed
But bringing justice and tolerance to my people
was my great need
I listened to their problems and concerns every day
And demonstrated that we should all live in the democratic way

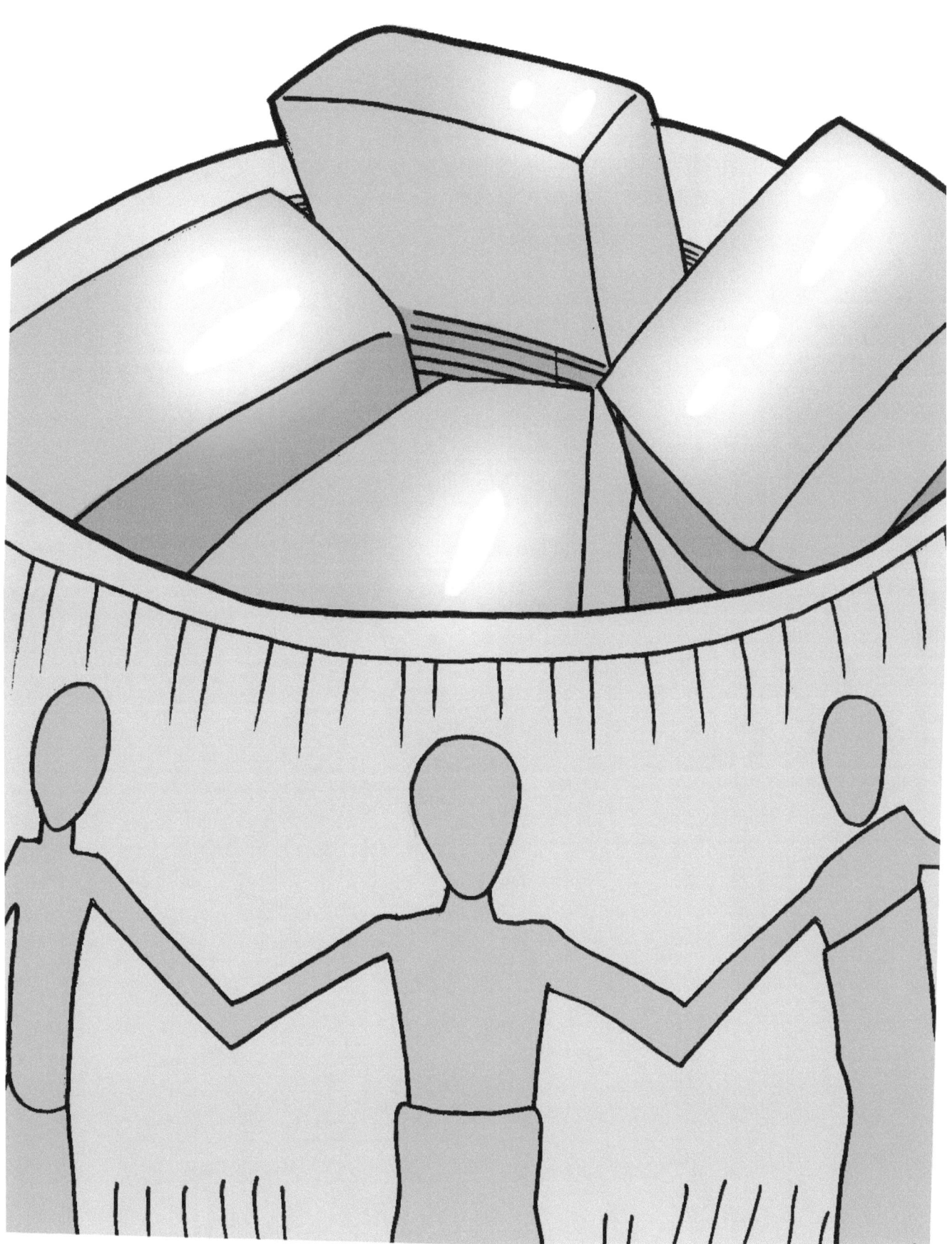

So as you can see, my dear readers, we share a very rich history.
Our ancestors were great kings and queens, pharaohs, and rulers in Africa.
They designed and built superb pyramids, temples, and statues to honor themselves.
Some of these edifices were: the Pyramid of Ghiza, The Steppe Pyramid,
and the Great Sphinx.
But let's take a closer look at Africa, at some of its countries,
and their cultures, their way of life, and their beliefs.

Let's start with ancient Egypt, or Kemet, which is its original name.
Because Egypt (Kemet) was such a fertile land, specifically near the Nile River,
many people came to live there, thousands of years ago.
The people who lived in Kemet were either farmers who grew crops, or noblemen,
who owned land and were more well off then the farmers.
And of course there were the kings and queens, or the Pharaohs.
The ancient people of Kemet wore Tunics, or white linen shirts,
which were cut to fit them.
The women's tunics usually went all the way down to their feet.
But, when the men went out to work in the fields,
they wore something like a short skirt called a kilt, which fit around their waists.

The people of Kemet believed in many gods,
and they worshipped these gods with animal sacrifices.
They believed that the Pharaoh was like a god,
and so the people had much respect for the Pharaoh.
To honor the pharaoh, the people built great pyramids,
columns, and other edifices. When the pharaoh died,
he, or she would be buried in these pyramids,
or tombs, along with their favorite foods and precious clothes and jewelry.
You see, the pharaoh and the people believed in an after life (that they would live again),
so they made sure that the pharaoh had every thing she, or he needed in the afterlife.

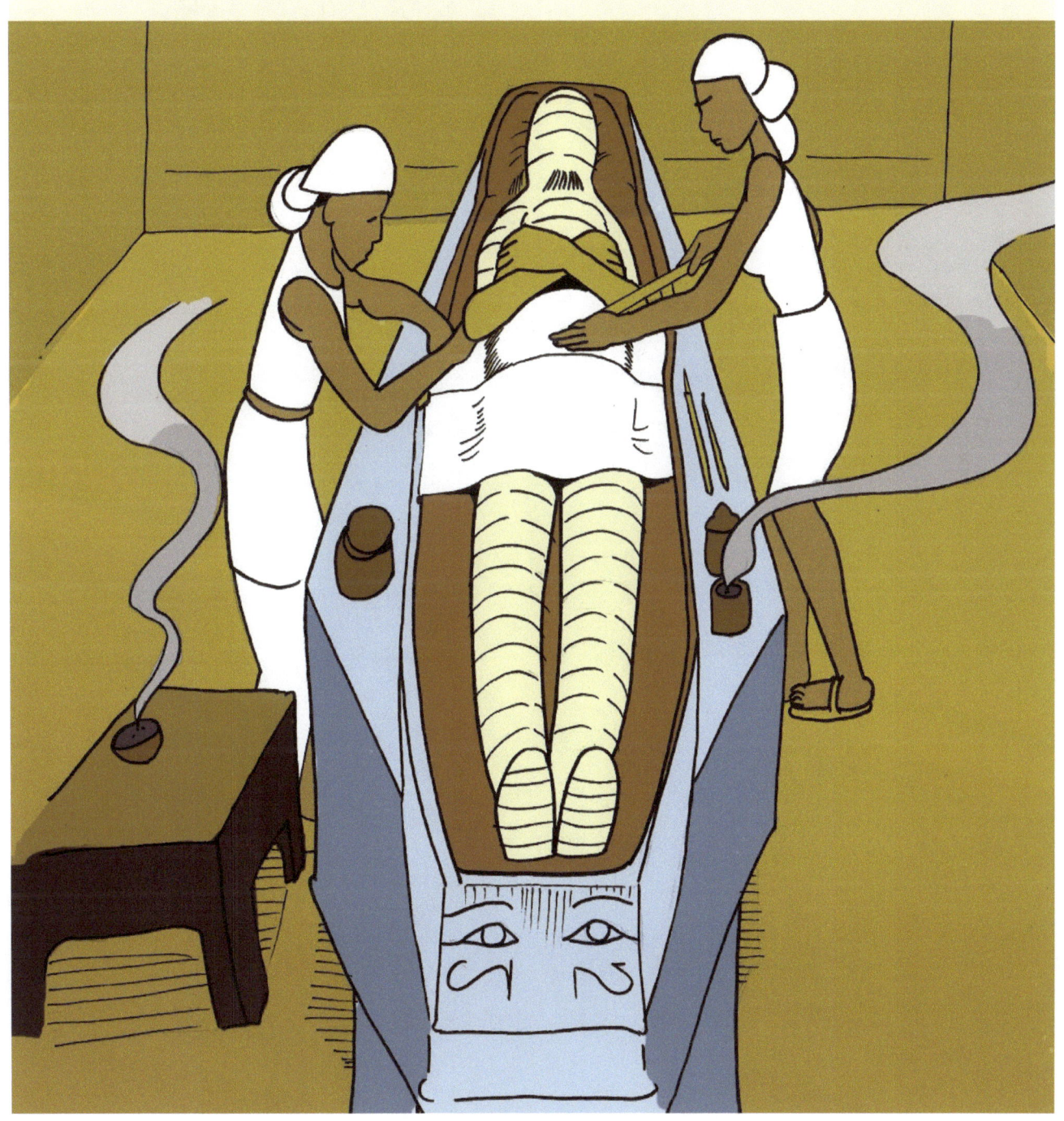

The people of Kemet also believed in living righteous lives. There were Nine Cardinal Principals of Righteousness, or being right in ancient Kemet.

They are:
1. Right Intentions
2. Right Thoughts
3. Right Speech
4. Right Effort
5. Right Action
6. Right Living
7. Right Reality
8. Right Understanding
9. Right Wisdom

Living by these rules encouraged the people of Kemet to always seek the highest good and to live in peace with one another.

A typical day in the life of a person living in Kemet would be, for example, a nobleman would get up, wash and dress in a kilt (a kilt is like a short skirt that men wore), have bread and fruit for breakfast and be off to the fields to check on his workers and his crops.

The wife would get up, wash and dress, have a breakfast of bread and fruit, and have her children dressed and fed, and brought to her by the servant. The wife would spend the day grinding wheat and making bread, while the children played.

Farmers had a similar lifestyle, only, they had to work in the fields themselves, and they usually did not have servants to help them.

Also a farmer's home, furniture, and clothing were not as fancy as that of the nobleman.

Farmers lived a much simpler life, but they were happy.

In many African cultures, the woman was very highly respected.
Many African communities were headed by women, who were usually very wise and strong willed.
One example is Queen, Pharaoh Hatshepsut, who was appointed by her father
to be the chief aide and heiress to the throne of Egypt.
Hatshepsut built many beautiful temples and pyramids, which are a tribute to her sense of beauty, creativity and strength.
Today she is still known as "The Ablest Queen of Far Antiquity."

One of the most famous Egyptians (persons of Kemet) was Imhotep. Although Imhotep was not of royal blood, or royal status, his many accomplishments landed him a very revered name in history, and also catapulted him to a god-like status.
Imhotep is known throughout Egypt, as 'The Father of Medicine.'
Imhotep is known to have diagnosed 200 diseases:
diseases of the abdomen,
bladder, skin, hair, and many, many other areas of the body.

He performed surgery, practiced dentistry,
and developed many medicines from plants.
This incredible genius of a man was also an architect, a scribe (one who writes things by hand on papyrus paper),
a high priest, a sage, a poet, an astrologer, and an adviser to King Djoser (who reigned from 2630-2611 BC),
the second king of Egypt's third dynasty.

One of Imhotep's greatest accomplishments is the design and the building of the very first pyramid; the Steppe Pyramid.
Today, the Steppe Pyramid is known as one of the most brilliant architectural wonders of the world.
Imhotep may have been born a commoner, but he is historical proof, that with genius, ability, and hard work, you can accomplish much in life.

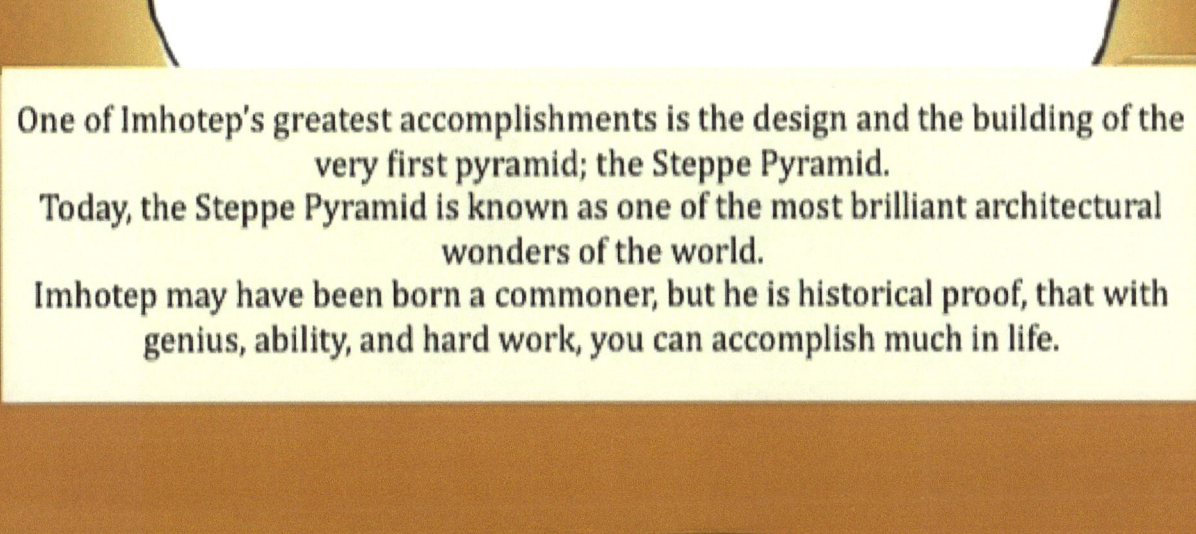

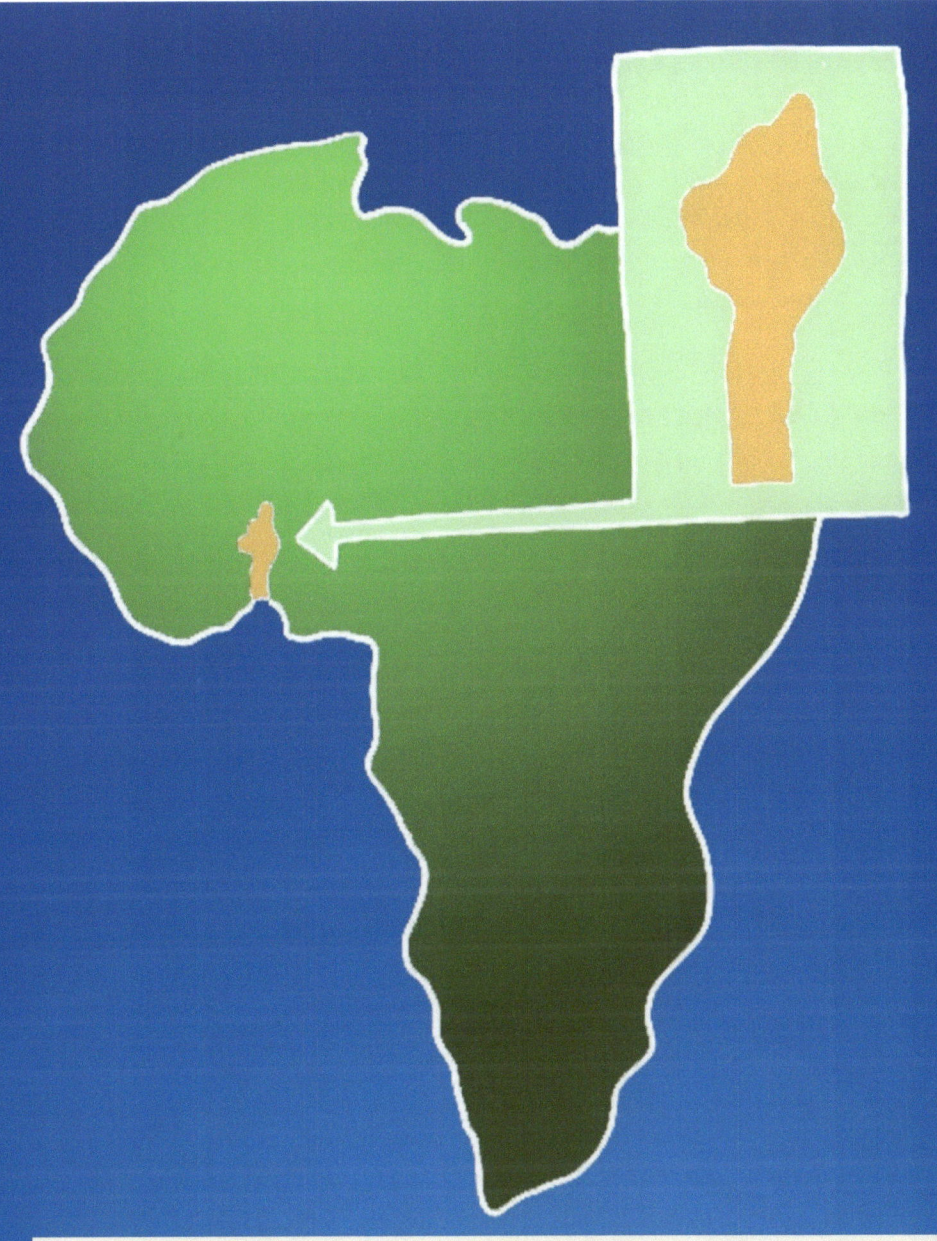

Well, Let's travel west from Egypt over Libya and Algeria,
and drop down south to Togo and Ghana, and there we will find Benin
sandwiched between Ghana and Togo.
Although Benin is a pretty small country, compared to many
other African countries, it has a glorified history.
The ancient Kingdom of Benin existed way back in the BCE times
and enjoyed centuries of prosperity and happiness until the 1800's.
The people of Benin created some of the most beautiful art and
bronze pieces in the world. Countries all over the world traded with
Benin for the magnificent art they offered. Some other types of workers
in Benin were: witchdoctors, warriors, magicians, farmers, weavers,
builders, and storytellers.

A king, who was assisted by a council of very intelligent and important people in the kingdom, led the government of Benin. The council represented the people, and the people in the kingdom worked together and helped each other, so that life was happy and good. Benin had a very strong army that was ready to fight when necessary. However, their leaders were wise and the people worked together, so most of their times were very peaceful. The children did not go to school like today, but rather were taught at home by their parents. Parents taught their children and other children in the area, different trades.
Parents also used various proverbs to teach their children right from wrong. The children learned how to become good citizens from watching their parents. Here we can see how the "Village" took care of its own.

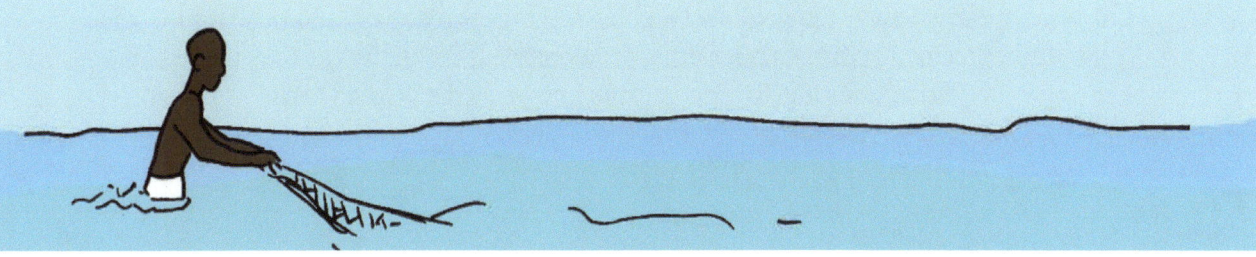

Now, let's move over one country to the left: to the country of Ghana.
The ancient kingdom of Ghana was actually located about 400 miles northwest,
of the modern day Ghana of today.
You see, the modern day Ghana won it's freedom from the British and decided
to take the name of the ancient country of Ghana.
An intelligent council of elders assisted the king who ruled Ghana.
Rules were created to maintain peace and order, and the people followed the rules.
The people of Ghana were farmers, miners, and artists.
They created beautiful clothes called Kente Cloth, by using different dyes and mud.
The Ghanaians were very happy people, and why shouldn't they be?
They lived close to the River Niger, so they had plenty of water,
which they used to farm, cook, and clean with.
They had many fruits and vegetables to grow and eat,
and they of course had the river to catch fish. Life was good!

Children did not go to school as they do today in Ghana, either.
Instead, they would get together at night, around a big fire and listen to the Griot (the story teller of the village) tell wonderful stories. You may have heard of Anansi the Spider.
Well, stories about Anansi were some of the childrens' favorites.
These stories always ended with a moral, or an important lesson about life.
Ghana became a very rich country, by controlling the trade of salt and gold,
which had to pass by Ghana's coastline, in order to reach the other countries.
The king of Ghana made a deal with the traders; they could pass by Ghana safely and trade,
if they only carried away the gold dust and left the bigger rocks of gold behind in Ghana.
For this agreement, Ghana's huge army would protect the traders as they passed by.
Because of this, Ghana became known as the "Gold Coast."

In Africa, our ancestors hunted and fished for food.
They grew crops in the field to feed their families.
They made their own clothing with beautiful,
bright colored cloth.
The men and women made beautiful pottery,
vessels and containers of all shapes, sizes, and colors.
Africans were the first to melt iron into ore:
creating marvelous swords and many other iron utensils.

Not only were the wonderfully crafted utensils, dishes, and weapons present throughout the African nations, but they were also found in Mexico. Mexico you say? Yes, Mexico! Apparently, African people visited America before it was called America, before Columbus sailed to the "New World." Actually, Africans had sailed to Mexico thousands of years before Columbus was born.
The Africans lived and worked with the Native Americans of Mexico.
They shared their culture and knowledge with them.
Many statues and sculptures were left behind;
statues that clearly show features of black men.
The Olmecs of Mexico is one such tribe that has many artifacts
(masks, statues, totem poles, etc.), which prove that black people,
African people were definitely present in America.
Say! That also proves that Africans were also great navigators!!

But what became of these great nations, kings, queens, and peoples?

Although the great empires of Africa flourished for thousands of years, eventually their enemies nearby and far away defeated them. Some came from Assyria, some from Arabia, and some came from as far away as Europe and America.

African lands were defeated, destroyed, and Europeans searching for gold and other precious materials took the African people as slaves. First, the Arabs took Africans to Asia. Much later, when the Europeans saw how strong, vibrant, trusting and friendly the Africans were, they decided to capture these trusting people, and carry them off to Europe and America, to use them as slaves.

Sad to say, Africans, greedy for the things of the world, helped to sell some of their own people into slavery.

Once Africans were taken from their homes and put in chains, they were forced to make the treacherous trek from Africa's interior to the western coast of Africa.
Here, the unfortunate people were locked in dungeons, where they waited for weeks, months, and even sometimes for a year or more.
Half of the Africans did not even make it across the vast land to the west coast. Many died of starvation, ill treatment, and horrible living conditions.

Once the Africans were finally taken from the slave castles and put aboard the slave ships headed for the Caribbean and the Americas, the worst part of their voyage was about to begin; the "Middle Passage."

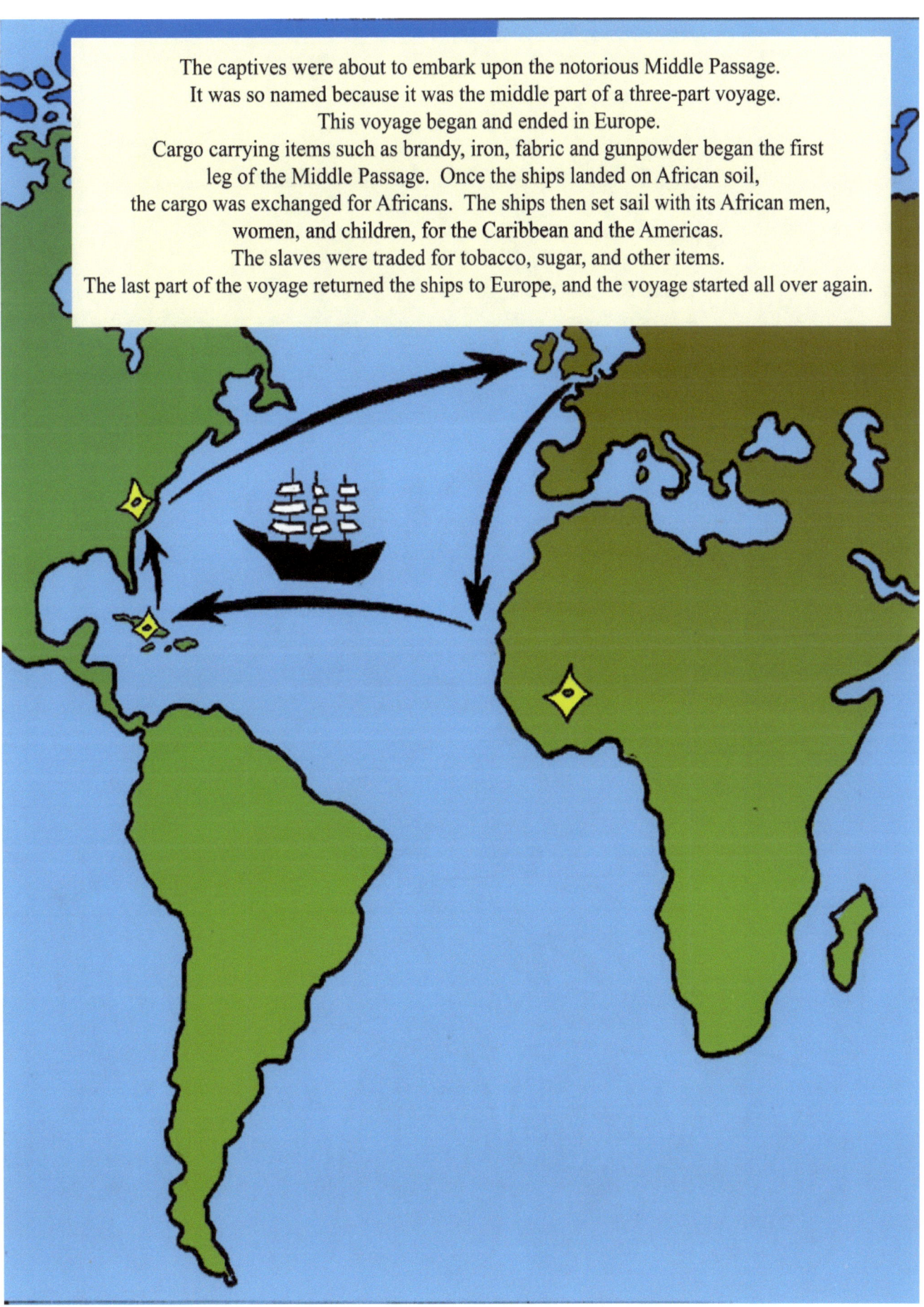

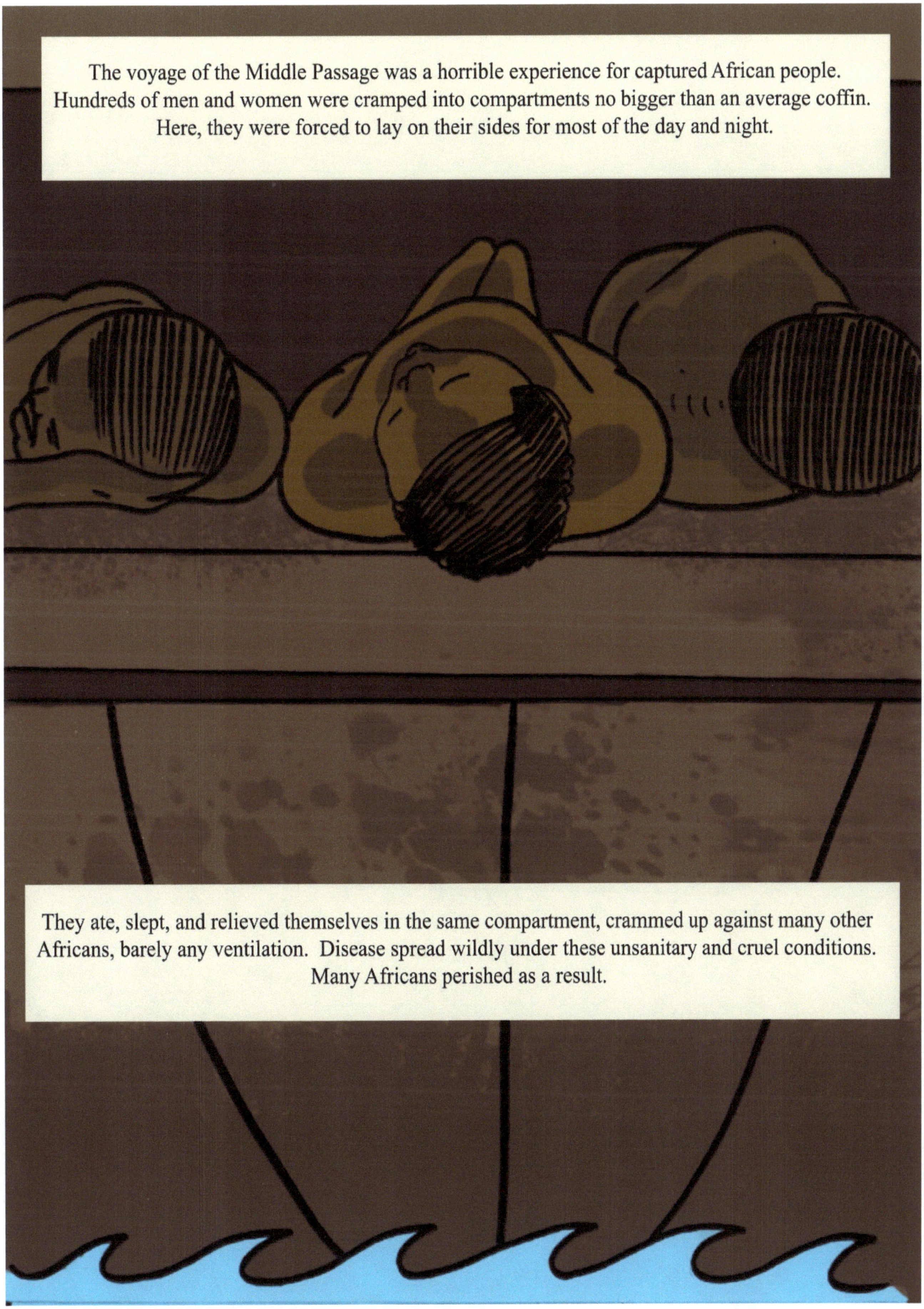

Many Africans would rather die, than succumb to such inhumane treatment. When they refused to eat, they were forced to eat with the help of a machine called the speculum orum, which held the mouth open. Many Africans took their lives, by jumping overboard into the deep blue sea. They would rather die, than live a life of maltreatment, as a slave.

Once the slave ships landed in the Americas (South and Central America were the first homes for slaves in America), they were finally bathed, greased (to improve their appearance), and taken to the slave auction blocks, where they were sold to the highest bidders.

The life of the African slave was a very tough one.
Slaves lived in small cabins with dirt floors, and very little heat,
and most cabins had no windows.
Therefore, the cabins were very hot in the summer and very cold in the winter.
These living quarters had little or no furniture and the Africans slept on a thin mat,
placed on the dirt floor. A slave had no more than two sets of clothing to wear and
he wore them until they were much worn. Only then did a slave receive a new set of clothing.
Most slaves did not own a pair of shoes.

African slaves worked long hours under the scorching hot sun, planting and picking sugar cane, tobacco, and later on cotton in North America. Most Africans worked twelve hours or more in the fields, with a very little break to eat or to rest. If the slave complained, or was not working fast enough, he was often beaten with a whip, and called terrible names by the overseer. The overseer was the person in charge of watching the slaves, assigning them work, and making sure they worked hard and long in the fields. Africans worked under these very cruel conditions and were not paid any wages for their labor.

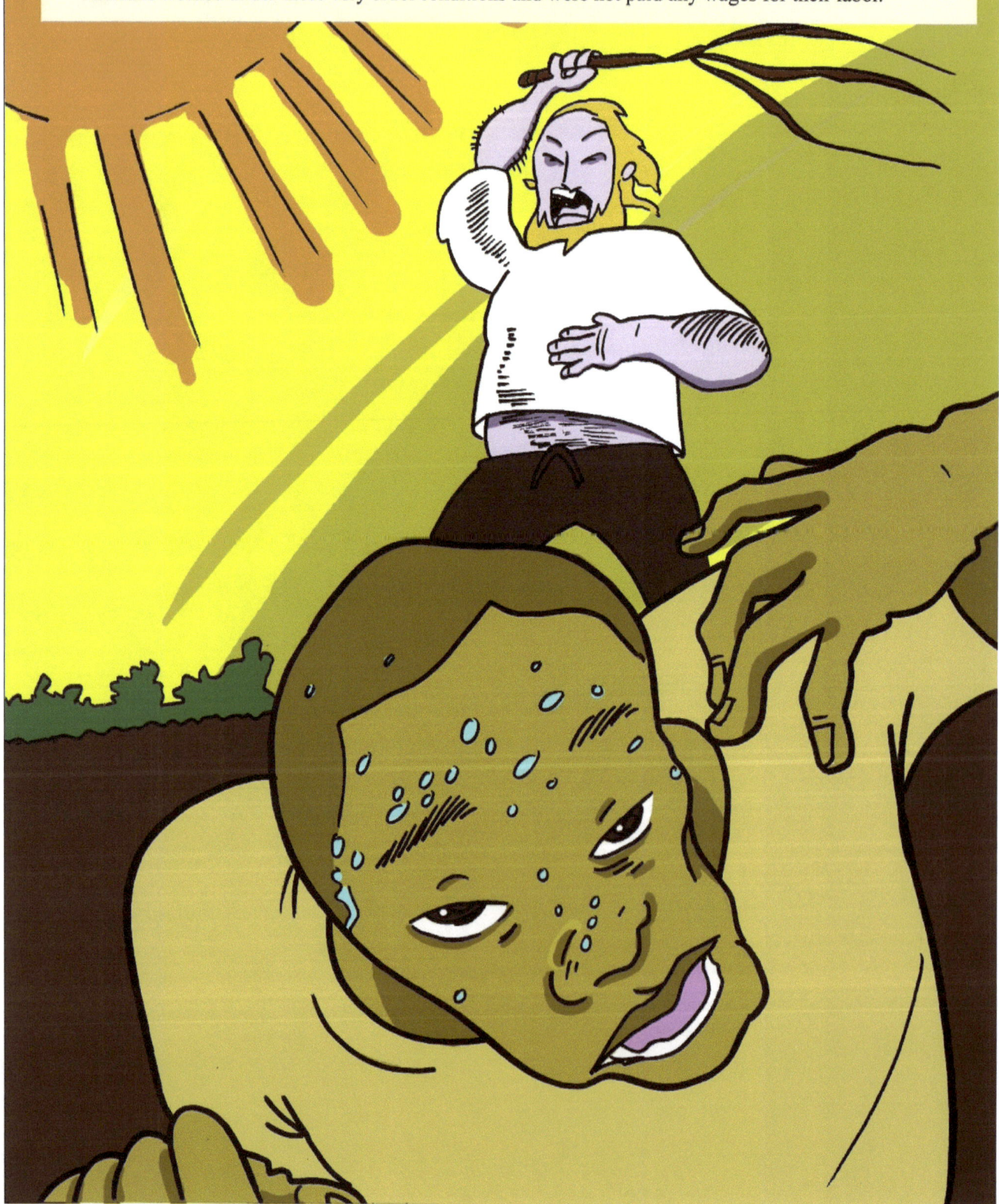

There were some slaves that also worked in the master's house, or "The Big House."
In the Big House, the Africans cooked, cleaned, washed clothes,
cared for the master's children, and handled many other affairs of the house hold.
They made sure the master's house ran smoothly.
Although these house slaves did not have to labor under the scorching,
hot sun, as the "field hands" did, they were also often beaten if their work did not please the master.

African slaves were forbidden to read, or write.
It was against the law for a slave to be educated.
The masters knew that if the Africans learned how to read,
write, and figure (do math), they would become educated and figure out ways to
escape and to end slavery. The masters were right!
An educated man is a dangerous man, for he will not be satisfied with the crumbs
that fall from his master's table.
Oh no! He will try to advance himself in life so that he can create his Own Home
with his OWN TABLE! So we see that education was important back then.
So important, that it was withheld from the African for four hundred years during slavery.
So how important should it be to you today?

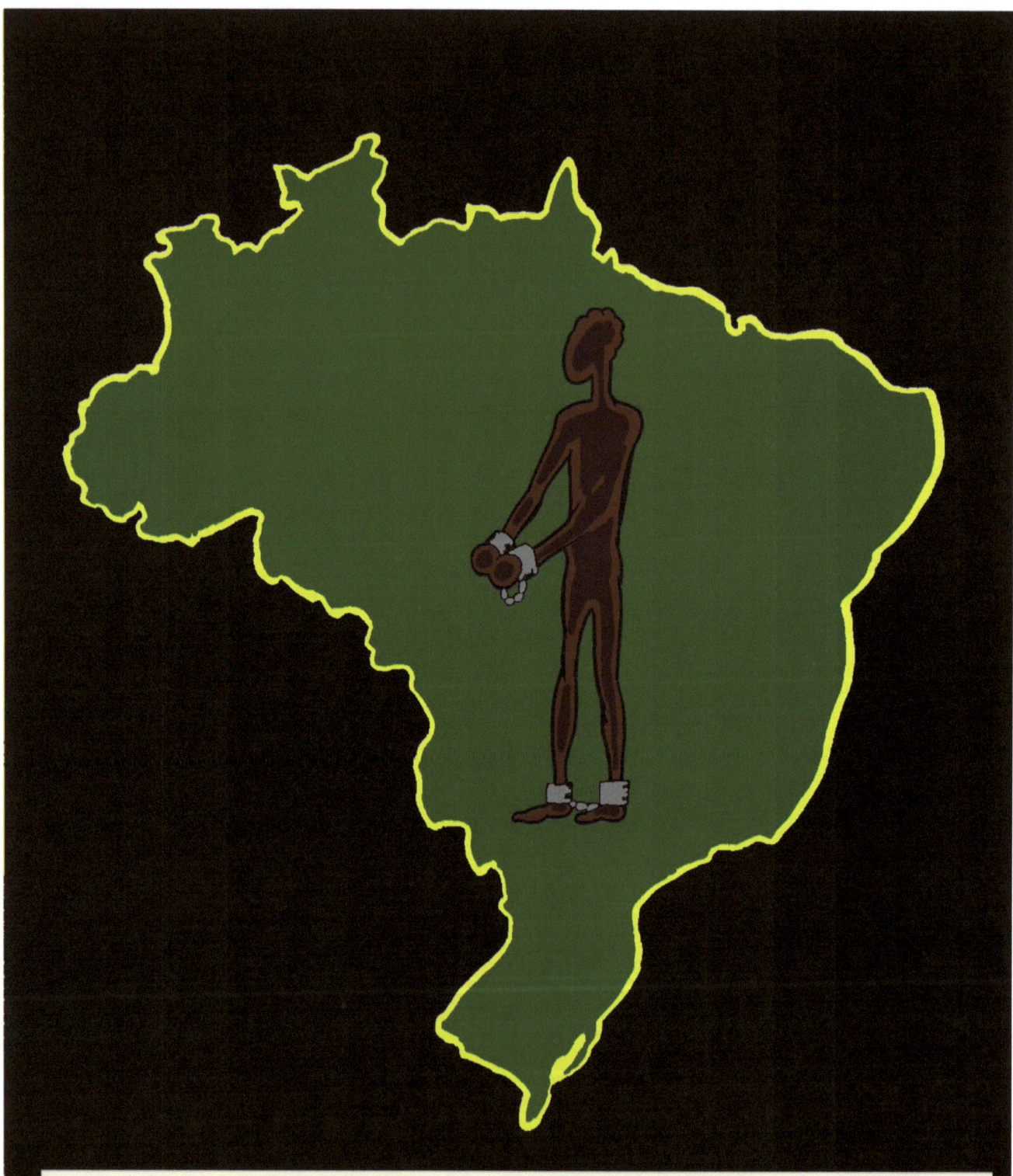

Twelve million Africans were shipped to the Americas from the 16th to the 19th century. About 645,000 of these were brought to what is now the United States. Most of them were shipped to Brazil. The slave population in the United States had grown to four million by the 1860 Census.

Contrary to what most people may think, slavery did not just exist in the South. It existed in the following states: Virginia, West Virginia, North Carolina, South Carolina, Georgia, Florida, Tennessee, Alabama, Louisiana, Delaware, Missouri, Mississippi, Kentucky, Texas, and the District of Columbia. It in fact started in the New England states of the North: Rhode Island, Connecticut, Massachusetts, New York, New Jersey and Pennsylvania. African slaves were living in all of these states, a generation before slavery was legalized in the South.

African slaves in the North typically worked as coachmen, footmen, artisans, house slaves, and valets. They also worked in factories and mills.

During the revolutionary war, the British promised Africans their freedom, if they fought on their side.
Thousands of slaves did escape and fought with the British and were given their freedom after the war. Because of this, the North lost many slaves and soon was forced to give up slavery altogether.

In the South, slavery flourished and southerners saw no reason to give up this very profitable institution. During all of these years of slavery, many, many slaves attempted and succeeded in escaping slavery. One such person was the notable Harriet Tubman. As a young girl, she hated slavery and promised herself that one day; she would escape to the North and be free.

The newly freed Africans were overjoyed at finally being free.
But there were many challenges ahead. Remember now, they had been slaves all of their lives,
living on the various farms, plantations, and dwellings of their former masters.
They had no home to call their own.
They had never worked for any one except their owners.
In addition to these stifling circumstances, the African slaves, now set free,
had never been allowed to learn to read or write.
How then, would they make a life for themselves, with no formal education,
no money and no home?

Well, some newly "freedmen" decided to remain on the farms,
or plantations with their former slave masters.
They were given a place to stay and some seed, and utensils to grow their own crops.
In return, they would repay the owners by giving them either part of the money they would earn
during the harvest, or a portion of the crops grown on the plot of land they now lived on...
This arrangement was known as "sharecropping."

It sounded like a great idea, but in reality, it was another form of slavery.
You see, the sharecropper had to buy on credit; tools, food, seed, and clothing,
from the farm owner, or the town merchant.
By the time the crop was harvested, and the sharecropper gave half of his crop to the land
owner, and paid back the money he'd borrowed, he usually was left with little,
or nothing for his family, and usually fell into debt; always owing more than he earned.

Many other freedmen decided to move on and take their chances in a new part of the country. The Freedman's Bureau, a government run organization was set up to assist the freedmen with food, clothing, shelter, and jobs.
The bureau was also set in place to protect the rights of the newly freed men.
At one point, the U.S. government even promised every newly freed family
40 acres and a mule, to help them get on their feet and start new lives.

This promise is known as reparations, for the hundreds of years that blacks suffered in slavery in the U.S. However, the government never made good on that promise.
And to this day, the expression "40 acres and a mule," is a reminder to African Americans, that the U.S. government never kept its promise.

African Americans had bigger worries, than the government's broken promise of 40 acres and a mule. You see, there were many Whites, in the south that hated the idea of Blacks now being free; and though they were now free, Whites would try everything in their power to make sure that they were NOT equal. This was the time of reconstruction of the South, the rebuilding of the South. New homes and businesses had to be built, schools were also started to educate Black children.
Some White people thought that too much was being done for the Blacks.
A terrorist group called the Ku Klux Klan (the KKK) was started in the South.
Farmers, businessmen, and even lawmakers, put on white sheets, and white hoods, and rode around at night, attacking and terrorizing innocent Black families.

These hate crimes were committed against Blacks throughout the south.
Black families were attacked at night, their homes were often set on fire,
while black men were dragged from their homes, beaten,
tortured (some were beaten to death, others were whipped senseless,
still others were hanged, and or burnt alive).
These were terrible times for black people, who were only trying to make an honest living,
surviving in a very hostile environment.

But the Black man is a strong man, and he fell back on his faith in God to see him through the worst of times.
He persevered, and through these turbulent times, he survived.

African Americans survived the reconstruction era, a very trying,
turbulent, and dangerous time in American History.
Eventually, Blacks became more educated and were able to get better jobs.
A small minority of Blacks, those who were able to attend college,
were now members of the middle class.
These Blacks were doctors, lawyers, clergymen, and scientist, to name a few.
They lived in nice homes, and had respectable positions in society.

However, the majority of Blacks still were living in poverty, barely making it. Whites in the North were not happy that Blacks were living beside them. Discrimination was practiced all over the North too, but segregation and discrimination were openly practiced in the South.

Laws were passed in the South to deny Blacks their rights.
These laws said that Blacks could not convene in large groups in town.
Blacks were expected to step aside when Whites approached them on the sidewalk.
They were expected to say "yassum" (meaning 'yes ma'm'), and "no-umm" (meaning 'no ma'm'); denoting themselves as less than intelligent people. Blacks were given ridiculous tests to pass,
in order to be able to vote. Restrooms and water fountains were segregated.
Blacks could only use those facilities that were labeled "Colored Only."
Blacks had to enter movie theaters from the rear of the building,
and also enter public buses from the rear.
Many restaurants would not serve Blacks at all,
and such was also true of most hotels and motels in the South.
These unfair laws or codes were part of the "Jim Crow" system of the South.

Hello Negro man, I am the Jim Crow Law.
I hear you're free!
Well, you may be free, but, don't walk through my neighborhood!
You may be free, but, don't send your kids to my school!

You may be free, but you're not welcome in My restaurant!
You may be free, but you must use THAT fountain and THAT restroom only!
Yeah, you may be free,
but just remember,
SEGREGATION IS THE RULE AROUND HERE!

Though the Negro (as African Americans were referred to at the time) was separated, and segregated, and discriminated against, and humiliated; he did not give in to this inhumane treatment. No, the Negro fought back with non - violent marches and sit-ins, demonstrations, and rallies, preaching, and prayers, appeals, and speeches.
They sat in at restaurant counters. They boycotted libraries.
They marched across bridges, and marched up court house steps; all the while, demanding their freedom;
the basic right of every human being, under the United States Constitution.
And for their many efforts of bravery and determination, they were stalked, and criticized, bullied and beaten, humiliated and hanged, stoned and stared at.
Dogs were sicked on them, fire hoses were sprayed on them, rocks and bottles were thrown at them, spit flew in their faces, and many innocent skulls were CRACKED! Blood, oozing onto the ground.
The ground, the land, which should have represented FREEDOM FOR ALL!

During this turbulent time in our history, names come to mind; names that represent men and women who fought the fight, and were not afraid to face the consequences which were sorrowfully attached to standing up for one's rights.
One of these individuals was Rosa Parks.
She really got the civil rights movement moving when she refused to give up her seat on a bus to a white man, in Montgomery Alabama. She was tired, and she was Fed Up!
Her courage motivated an entire city to stand up and walk, rather than ride the segregated buses.

Martin Luther King Jr., a young preacher at the time was chosen to lead the Montgomery Bus Boycott, in Alabama. King went from being virtually unknown, to becoming the voice of African Americans across the nation, crying out for freedom and justice.
The bus boycott was a great success, and after 381 days of not using the buses in Montgomery, and choosing to walk to work, or car pool,
African Americans won the right to sit anywhere they chose to on the city buses.
What Sweet Victory!

But King was just beginning the fight for freedom for Blacks and all other disenfranchised peoples. The next thirteen years found Martin Luther King, Jr. fighting for poor people's right to proper housing, better jobs and wages, fresh and decent food in neighborhood super markets, the right to vote, and the right to stay out of the Vietnam War, to name a few.
King traveled across the country and around the world, defending the rights of Blacks and poor people of all races.
He was arrested and thrown in jail many times for his protests, but that just made him more determined!

One of King's favorite quotes was:
"If a man does not have something he is willing to die for, than he has nothing to live for."
And true to his words, Martin Luther King Jr's life was cut short, by an assassin's bullet,
as he stood on the balcony of the Lorraine Hotel, in Memphis Tennessee, on April 4th, 1968.
Because of King's tireless effort in his fight for civil rights for Blacks,
the entire world was forced to open its eyes and acknowledge the unfair treatment that
Blacks were still living under.
His march on Washington in 1966, which involved over 200,000 people,
demonstrated to the world
that Blacks were tired of being "second class citizens."
His famous "I Have a Dream" speech, coupled with his later meeting with
President John F. Kennedy, paid off, and Blacks were finally granted the right to vote
in the USA.
We thank you, Martin Luther King Jr.!

Another fiery fighter for justice and freedom was none other than Malcolm X. Although Malcolm and Martin were fighting for the same rights for African Americans, their methods were totally different. While martin took up peaceful hands and marched across the country, Malcolm took up militant words and guns, if necessary.

Martin's words were: let's appeal to our oppressors through peaceful, passive resistance, while Malcolm's words were: fight for what's right, "By any means necessary!"

They both wanted the same thing, Freedom!

They just didn't agree on how to obtain it.

Malcolm organized a huge following amongst the Black Muslims, or the Nation of Islam.

His followers were taught to band together and supply their own needs, and not wait for the government to do so.

In addition, they were encouraged to live together, closely as a community, and to have weapons in order to protect themselves and their families.

In October of 1966, in Oakland California, Huey Newton and Bobby Seale founded the Black Panther Party for Self-Defense.
This group was greatly influenced by Malcolm X.
Their goal was to fight for the rights of Blacks and other minorities, as well as poor Whites.
The Panthers believed in protecting minority communities from the government, with guns and other weapons. They were fighting for the economic, political, and social freedom for all minorities and poor people in the US.
Many people joined the Black Panther party.
Poor people and especially African Americans began to feel a sense of pride and power in knowing that there was a powerful force behind them;
supporting them in their fight for freedom.

Black Panthers such as Fred Hampton, a 21 year old, organized breakfast programs in places like Chicago and New York. These programs helped to feed thousands of poor children in the inner - cities. Medical centers were also started, as well as door - to door health care programs which offered free tests for sickle cell.
In addition, blood drives were started to aid the Cook County Hospital in Chicago.
These are just a few of many programs, which were started by the Black Panther Party.

The Reverend Al Sharpton, and Reverend Jesse Jackson, were just two of many more African Americans who championed the rights of poor minorities across the USA. Jesse Jackson worked with Martin Luther King Jr. in his early days, in Chicago. He started the program "Operation Push." Through this program, Jesse made it possible for blacks in Chicago to receive jobs in their own communities, to buy foods that were no longer spoiled, but actually fresh and worthy of human consumption, in their neighborhood stores.

He fought for safe and decent housing for the community, and he inspired thousands of school children to stay in school and study hard.

Here is an affirmation that Jesse started, and which I embellished.

I Am--- Somebody!
I Am--- Somebody!
I may be African American
I may be Caucasian
I may be Hispanic
I may be Native American
I may be Caribbean
I may be Arabian
I may be Hebrew,
But I Am--- Somebody
I Am--- Somebody!
I am---Somebody!
I may be young---
But I AM--- SOMEBODY!!!

Yes, my friends, you are Somebody!
Each one of you is somebody, intelligent, smart, creative, inquisitive, dynamic, and full of promise.
Just like the thousands of ancestors before you, such as: inventors like Benjamin Banneker who
invented the first clock in the US. He was an accomplished astronomer and a great mathematician.
Ben Bradley invented the steam engine and Dr. Charles Drew, the Blood Bank.

Some of our great civil rights leaders were Mary McLeod Bethune, and Linda Brown;
whose parents spearheaded the famous lawsuit,
"Brown verses the board of Education of the city of Topeka Kansas".
Frederick Douglass, Homer Plessey, Sojourner Truth and Elenor Holmes are just a few
of the many more leaders who fought for our freedom.

Some of our dynamic lawyers were Thurgood Marshall, Supreme Court judge, civil rights advocate, and one of the lawyers who argued on the Brown verses the Board of Education trial, Percy Sutton and Johnnie Cochran.

Educators who helped build a strong foundation for you and me are W. E. B. Dubois, John Hope Franklin, historian and educator, and Carter G. Woodson, a historian, educator, author and publisher, who started the practice of Black History Week, which eventually evolved into Black History Month.

The world of entertainment would not be what it is today, without some very talented individuals, such as James Earl Jones, Lauryn Hill, Diana Ross, Michael Jackson, Gladys Knight, Pattie La Belle, Tupac Shakur, The Supremes, The Temptations and so many, many more.
Musicians such as Scott Joplin, Louis Armstrong, Miles Davis, and Alicia Keys, to name a few, have inspired many young artists today.

And what would the sports playing field look like without the great players and athletes like Jesse Owens, who set a world record in the running broad jump (also called long jump), that stood for 25 years, and who won four gold medals in the 1936 Olympic Games in Berlin. Athletes such as Magic Johnson, Michael Jordan, Venus Williams, Serena Williams, and Lynette Woodard, a professional basketball player who made history in 1985, when she became the first female member of the Harlem Globetrotters, have motivated many youth today to follow their dreams.

Our writers have produced some of the most thought provoking, intriguing, motivating and inspiring works of our times. Nikki Giovanni, James Baldwin, Gordon Parks, James Weldon Johnson, Jacob Lawrence, Gwendolyn Brooks, Maya Angelou, Langston Hughes, Toni Morrison, Richard Wright, Spike Lee and Zora Neale Hurston, are just a few of many such important artists.

And let's not forget our politicians who have fought to secure our rights to life, liberty, and the pursuit of happiness. Men and women such as, Barbara Jordan, Shirley Chisholm, David Dinkins the first Black mayor of New York City, Patricia Roberts Harris, a politician, lawyer, educator and former ambassador to Luxembourg, Eric Holder, David Patterson, the first African American governor of New York State and Charles Rangel, a member of Congress, who has served 19 terms in the House of Representatives.

Many entrepreneurs (business men and women) have paved the way for our people to invest in, own, and manage their own businesses. Some of these people are Suzanne De Passé', who is partly responsible for the discovery of the Jackson 5. She is currently the CEO of her own TV production studio.
Berry Gordy created Motown Records Company, and also was responsible for the successful careers of many artists, such as Michael Jackson, The Supremes and Diana Ross.

Percy Sutton, a lawyer, businessman and activist represented Malcolm X,
and Russell Simmons founded Def Jam Records.
He was partly responsible for the spread and production of Hip Hop music.
Oprah Winfrey, the world's richest black woman today, owns her own T.V. network.
And Tyler Perry owns his own Movie and T.V. studio.

And of course, we have to take pride in the fact that Barak Hussein Obama,
a Chicago lawyer and senator, became the first African American President of the
United States of America. He knew he could do it, and so can you.
YES, YOU CAN!!!!

African Holocaust Society. African Kings and Queens - Akhenaton (1375- 1358 B. C.) http://www.africanlegends.info/. n.p. n.d.

Africans in America. The Middle Passage 1600 - 1800. http://www.pbs.org/wgbh/aia/part1/1p277.html. WGBH PBS online. n.d.

Anheuser-Busch Inc. St. Louis, MO. Copyright 1998. Great Kings and Queens of Africa. http://egyptsearchreloaded.proboards.com/thread/72. April 6, 2010.

Barton, Paul. "Black Civilizations of Ancient America (Muu-Lan), Mexico (XI): Gigantic Stone Head of Negritic African During the Olmec (Xi) Civilization." http://www.raceandhistory.com/historicalviews/ancientamerica.htm. Education. n.d.

Barton, Paul. "The Olmecs: An African Presence in Early America." http://www.theperspective.org/olmecs.html. The Perspective. February 28, 2001.

Bey, Umar, R. S. "First Americans Washutaw Muurs: When the Earth Was Called Muur Le Muria." www.4EverMaAT.com. Dec. 16, 2007.

Biography.com. Al Sharpton. Biography. http://www.biography.com/people/al-sharpton-207640. A+ E Television Networks, LLC. Sept. 28, 2011.

Biography.com. "Malcolm X. Biography." http://www.biography.com/people/malcolm-x-9396195. A+ E Television Networks, LLC. 1996-2013.

Bryant, Jonathan, M. Georgis Southern University. "Ku Klux Klan in the Reconstruction Era." New Georgia Encyclopedia. http://www.georgiaencyclopedia.org/nge/Article.jsp?id=h-694. Oct. 3, 2002.

Deviller Donegan Enterprises. Egypt's Golden Empire: A Day in the Life of. http://www.pbs.org/empires/egypt/special/lifeas/nobleman.html. n.p. March 15, 2006.

Equiano, Olaudah. The Middle Passage: Extracts From the Interesting Narrative. http://www.brycchancarey.com/equiano/extract3.htm. n.p. January 27, 2003.

Garifuno: "Black Carib Culture." http://www.clas.ufl.edu/users/afburns/afrotrop/garifuna.htm. n.p. n.d.

Gill, N. S. What Clothing Did the Ancient Egyptians Wear? About.com. http://ancienthistory.about.com/od/egyptwomen/f/102709EgyptianClothing.htm. n.d.

Hebert, Keith, S. University of West Georgia. " Ku Klux Klan in Alabama After the Reconstruction Era." http://www.encyclopediaofalabama.org/face/Article.jsp?id=h-2934. Encyclopedia of Alabama. Sept. 14, 2010.

Herbstein, Manu. Ama, a Story of the Atlantic Slave Trade: The Middle Passage. -http://www.ama.africatoday.com/middle_passage.htm. E. Reads. 2003.

Kunjufu, Jawanza Lessons From History: A Celebration in Blackness. Jr. - Sr. High Edition. African American Images: Chicago, Illinois. 1987.

McDonough, Yona Zeldis. Who was Harriet Tubman? New York, NY: The Penguin Group. 2002.

Meadows, James. Jesse Jackson. Chanhassen, MN. The Child's World, Inc. 2001.

Mrdonn.org. Ancient African Kingdom of Ghana. http://africa.mrdonn.org/ghana.htm. n.p. n.d.

Mrdonn.org. Ancient African Kingdom of Benin. http://africa.mrdonn.org/benin.html. n.p. n.d.

Nubianem: The History of the African Olmecs: Black Civilizations of America From Prehistoric Times.
----The Truth About the Ownership, Settlement, and Ancient Civilizations of Black African-Americans in the Americas Before Columbus. http://originalblacksofamericabeforecolumbus.blogspot.com/2005/11/blog-post.html. Blogger. Nov. 05, 2005.

Penn Museum. Egyptian Pharaohs. http://www.penn.museum/documents/education/pennmuseum_egypt_previsit_combined.pdf. n.p n.d.

Rosenberg, Jennifer. 100 Famous African American Men and Women of the 20th Century. http://history1900s.about.com/od/people/tp/famousafricanamericans.htm. n.p. n.d.

Sundiata, Acoli. "A Brief History of the Black Panther Party and Its Place in the Black History Movement." www.slideshare.net/.../a-brief-history-of-the-black-panther-party-positive... n.p. July 14, 2012.

The British Museum. Egyptian Life. http://www.ancientegypt.co.uk/life/home.html. n.p. n.d.

The Henry Ford. Rosa Parks: "The Story Behind the Bus." http://www.thehenryford.org/exhibits/rosaparks/story.asp. n.p. 2002.

Thompson, James, C. "Women in Ancient Egypt." http://www.womenintheancientworld.com/women_in_ancient_egypt.htm. n.p. n.d.

Wikipedia the Free Encyclopedia. African American History. https://en.wikipedia.org/wiki/African-American_history. 2011.

Wikipedia the free Encyclopedia. Slavery in America. https://en.wikipedia.org/wiki/Slavery_in_the_United_States. 2010.

Winters, Clyde, A. Africans Came Before Columbus. Evidence of African Presence in Ancient America. Euro Africa- Magazine Website. http://www.bibliotecapleyades.net/arqueologia/olmecs01.htm. n.d.

Wormser, Richard. The Rise and Fall of Jim Crow. Reconstruction 1865-1877. http://www.pbs.org/wnet/jimcrow/stories_events_reconstruct.html. n.p. n.d.--

Janice G. Logan is a native of Brooklyn, New York,
who currently resides in a small suburban town of Atlanta, Georgia.
She and her husband moved there in 1993, with their four children,
and have been living there ever since.
They have eight beautiful grandchildren.
Janice is an elementary school teacher,
who loves to read,
and encourages her students to become life-long readers.

From Pyramids, to Poverty, to Pride is Janice's first children's book.
It began as a play 20 years ago, and over time, evolved into a book.

Janice says,
*"When we were growing up, we did not have much information about our history,
or our heritage.
The most I learned in school was that our people were slaves.
I learned of Harriet Tubman and Crispus Attucks, and that was about it.
I want African American children to know,
and be very proud of their heritage, who they truly are,
what their people have done,
and how they can positively contribute to society.
We truly have an extraordinary history and I want every child to know that.
That is why I created this book. "*

**ADOFO works out of Atlanta, GA
and North Carolina
showcasing his art @
http://adofosart.storenvy.com/
https://www.facebook.com/artbyAdofo**

www.ingramcontent.com/pod-product-compliance
Lightning Source LLC
Chambersburg PA
CBHW042035150426
43201CB00002B/27